Instagram Marketing

Growing Your Instagram Following And Turning Them Into Profitable Customers For Your Business Through Selling and Affiliate Marketing.

Brad Tiller

© Copyright 2018 - All rights reserved.

It is not legal to reproduce, duplicate, or transmit any part of this document in either electronic means or in printed format. Recording of this publication is strictly prohibited and any storage of this document is not allowed unless with written permission from the publisher except for the use of brief quotations in a book review.

Contents

Introduction 1

Chapter 1: The Value of Instagram 2
Chapter 2: Optimizing Your Profile 5
Chapter 3: Doing Your Research 9
Chapter 4: Your Image 13
Chapter 5: Marketing Through Images 21
Chapter 6: Getting Followers and Engagement 28
Chapter 7: Selling Your Product/Service Via Instagram 35
Chapter 8: Affiliate Marketing 39
Chapter 9: Other Social Media 43

Resources 44
Conclusion 45

Introduction

Congratulations on downloading *"Instagram Marketing"*! This book is a great find, and it will support you in making the most out of your Instagram business account.

If you are unfamiliar with Instagram marketing, this book will be extremely handy in helping you understand the ins and outs that you need to know to maximize your return on investment. From learning how to optimize your profile to understanding how Instagram marketing works and exploring the value of gaining traffic, product selling and affiliate marketing. You will learn everything you need to know to start making money on Instagram in the shortest time possible.

Marketing is a continually changing field that is constantly being overrun by the latest and greatest trends that appeal to each businesses target audience. In this book, you are going to learn what the current trends are, as well as how you can stay on top of them as they continue to change. Through effective use of the app, you can stay ultra-relevant, maximize your following, and improve engagement on your account. As a result, you will directly maximize the amount of income you earn through your Instagram account.

For anyone who is unfamiliar with Instagram marketing, or if you are already fairly good at it but would love additional pointers, this book will be a great read for you. Everything you need to know is within these pages. All that's left for you to do is tap into them, access the information, and begin putting it into action! After that, you will begin seeing your return on investment skyrocketing. So, go ahead and get started! And of course, enjoy!

Chapter 1: The Value of Instagram

Instagram is a great marketing tool that brings significant value to both businesses and consumers. Whether you are already running a business, or still looking to start one based on Instagram, you can feel certain that you are going to receive great value from working on this platform.

Instagram claims to have over 800 million users. Of those users, 1/3 have reported using Instagram as a way to purchase products online. This means that approximately 266 million people have used Instagram to influence a purchasing decision and to purchase products directly through other app users. Instagram users are 70% more likely to purchase products online as a result of this application as compared to non-Instagram users. As you can see, Instagram has a great potential for creating and finalizing sales.

The potential to reach your target audience and facilitate sales directly through the application itself is massive. This means that Instagram not only allows you to increase your outreach and maximize your ability to reach your target audience but many individuals will actually purchase directly through your profile as well. Instagram is a great tool that allows you to market directly through the application and acquire great results from your efforts. Plus, it is entirely free unless you choose to take advantage of their paid advertisements.

If you do want to take advantage of Instagram's paid advertisements, they are said to have the most advanced social media advertising target options available in today's world. This means that you can get very specific on who your target consumers are and market directly towards them, maximizing your rate of return and making it easier than ever to make sales through this platform. Plus you can track their advertisement features, so you can clearly see how they are performing, which part of your audience is most interested, and how you can reach them better.

Another great feature on Instagram is that you can actually switch your personal profile into a business profile, granting you access to far more insightful features. These features allow you to understand exactly who your audience is and see how well your posts are performing. You can also use them to promote your page through paid advertisements and to add a large "email" button at the top of your profile that will encourage interested parties to contact you for more information about your products or services.

Instagram offers a great unique opportunity to build a profile through social media. This means that you can create a personable brand that interacts directly with your consumer, helping you build customer relationships. Customer relationships are one of the leading things driving individuals to purchase from companies, so having a platform that makes it extremely easy to build these relationships means that you are giving yourself direct access to great returns on your time and investment.

Lastly, Instagram is a great platform that allows you to directly understand your consumer. You can see what they are interested in, what they do not like, and where they are spending most of their time. You can understand their interests and the things they care about, discover what encourages them to purchase from people and learn how you can use visual appeal to attract them to your brand and encourage sales. Other platforms that lack visual aids are less convenient to market on since individuals love to "see" what they are buying before they commit. This means you can accomplish the visual aspect as well as the verbal aspect in one post, promoting and encouraging sales easier than ever before.

Instagram is a powerful tool that will amplify your ability to reach your audience. Furthermore, if you are just starting a business, you can use Instagram itself to create money without the use of any other platforms. In fact, you don't even need a website to get started. Using business models such as affiliate marketing, which you will learn more about in Chapter 6, will give you the ability to create passive money through Instagram with minimal effort and maximum results.

Bonus Factors about Instagram: Instragram stories are massive and you are able to link your Instagram posts to Facebook and Twitter so you do not have to post on each individual Social Media Account.

Chapter 2: Optimizing Your Profile

Optimizing your profile is an essential practice in making sure that you have an account that is going to serve you and your business well. Since Instagram has been around since 2010, we have a strong idea of what you need to have in place in order for your audience to find you, follow you, and consume anything you post.

Here is what you need to do to optimize your profile, maximize your following, and increase your outreach and sales through Instagram.

Create Your Profile
The first part of really taking advantage of Instagram is having an account! Creating your account is simple, but there are some things you need to consider if you want to optimize your account so that you can run a business with it!

Username
First, you need to pick your username. When you are creating a username for your business, it is important that you pick something that accurately reflects your business. It should also be short and simple. Refrain from using any form of punctuation in your username as this can make it more challenging for your audience to find you. You would also want to refrain from having your username too close to anyone else's. If they are too close, your traffic might end up on the other person's page instead of yours. Lastly, make sure you choose a username that is available to you across all social media platforms. This will ensure that you can drive your traffic to other social sharing sites and that they can easily find you anywhere you go. I've found that keeping your username simple with just one word instead

of adding, full stops, underscores, dashes, etc... will make it easier and more simple for your customers to remember your business username. For example if your business name is 2 or 3 words, just join it as one word.

Bio
Your bio is a space on your page that allows you to write a short introduction about your business that is 150 characters or less. This means you can insert a brief but catchy introduction regarding what you can offer and what people can expect when they scroll your page. It is important to take advantage of this spot and create a bio that will be catchy and attractive. You want your audience to see it and be instantly intrigued and eager to see what your posts are about. If you are unsure as to what you should write, consider leaving this space blank and check out what other competition profiles are saying about themselves. However it is most effective creating one to two sentences on what your business provides followed by 2 or 3 bullet points. Keeping it short and powerful, rather than a block of text is definitely a must if you want to draw and excite your viewers.

Link
Instagram allows you to post a single link on your profile. Naturally, this should be a link to your website. However, if you do not have one yet, you may prefer to post a link to your second most-used social sharing site. Alternatively, there are some companies that have developed platforms that allow you to post a single link on your Instagram page that will then take your followers to a landing page that

allows them to choose what else they want to see from you. On this landing page, you can add other social sharing sites as well as your website. Companies that offer services like this include ones like Linktree.

Point of Contact
Once you convert your page to a business page, which can be done during setup or in the settings section of your completed profile, you are also given the opportunity to include a point of contact and the address of your business. Your point of contact should include your email, so be sure to create a new and more professional email for your business if you do not have one yet. You can also add your phone number if there is one that your audience can reach you at. If you do not plan on having customers call you directly or you do not have a business number, you can skip adding your phone number. If you have a spot where your company can be physically seen, for example, a storefront, you can also include that address here so that your audience can find you locally if they choose to look.

Profile Picture
Your profile picture needs to be something professional and identifiable. The best picture for a company to use in their profile picture is a logo of their company. This begins to build brand awareness and makes it easy to remember so that when people scroll past your profile, they remember exactly who you are. If you do not have a logo yet, you can consider getting one made by a freelancer on Fiverr, Upwork, or 99 designs. Fiverr and Upwork tend to run on the cheaper side of things, allowing you to get your logo from $5-$10. On the other side 99 designs are more expensive, but it does allow you the opportunity to get a wide range of designs to choose from, and they tend to give outputs with higher quality.

Theme
Following a certain type of theme on your Instagram will draw viewers to be more intrigued towards what your Instagram page is about. Following a color theme or posting a Quote or Word every 2nd photo are examples of what some businesses do. You can easily set up colored backgrounds with quotes on Word Swag to make this easier.

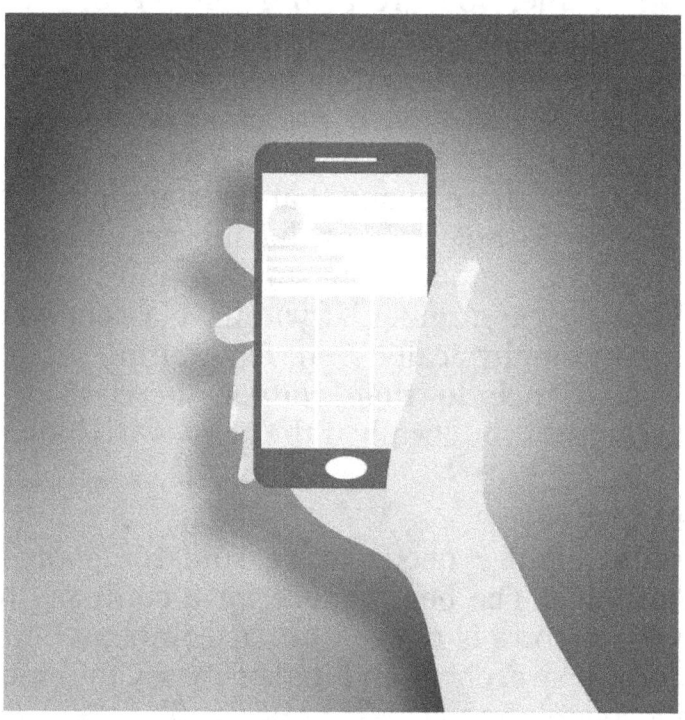

Chapter 3: Doing Your Research

Doing your research would have to be the most important step throughout the whole process. If done right you will be able to scale faster and keep your business running long term. You need to know your customers inside out and I will teach you how you can do this in the current chapter.

Researching Your Competition

Now that your profile is complete, you would want to begin researching what you are up against. Spending some time looking at your competition is a great way to discover what other people in your industry are doing to reach their target audience. If you have not yet written your bio, you can also pay attention to what their bios are saying so that you can choose one that is catchy and attractive and create your own, more intriguing version of it.

To research your competition, you can search for hashtags that are relevant to your niche on Instagram. Be sure to follow all of your competitors so you can stay up to date on what they are doing and get fresh and relevant information on how you can stay trending for your audience. You can also go to Google and begin to research your competition outside of Instagram. Search blogs, Facebook pages, twitter, forums, and other online platforms related to your niche. This will give you a strong idea of what is currently trending and how you can reach your audience better.

Paying attention to your audience is essential in staying relevant. Social media trends can change and start rapidly, often in a single afternoon or overnight. If you want to stay relevant for your audience, you need to stay on top of what they are interested in, where they are, and what they are doing. Following your competition and paying attention to your niche carefully allows you to recognize how fellow members of your niche are getting in on these trends. Then, you can combine their successful ideas with your own twist to develop your competitive edge.

It is important that you pay attention towards providing value and entertainment, so pay attention to how your competition is also doing this. When they are posting things that are providing value, what type of value are they offering? How are they sharing that value? Which pieces of value does your shared audience prefer the most? Additionally, when they are posting entertainment, pay attention to what they are posting. What does your audience find interesting or funny? What are they more likely to be attracted to? Being clear on the value and entertainment that your audience is interested in will support you in sharing posts that are on-target and that your audience is eager to consume.

Finding ideas of how popular pages in your niche are getting their audience engaged in posts is another crucial idea you need to look in to. Find the most Popular pages in your competition and get ideas from what they are doing while adding your own spice. The popular pages are popular for one reason and one reason only: They provide VALUE! Consistently.

Research Your Audience

While you are researching your competitors online, be sure to take some time to research your audience, too. Remember, these are the ones you are specifically targeting. Your competitors give you great insight and inspiration to reach your audience, but reaching your audience is the end goal. When you spend time on social sharing networks such as Instagram, you get a competitive edge because you are able to see your audience living their daily lives. You can follow them and engage with them online, which not only increases your brand awareness but also gives you the opportunity to understand what your audience cares about and what they are interested in. When you get to know your audience in this more intimate way, it becomes easier to understand what you should post to gain their awareness and attention.

Again, when you are researching your audience, take the time to discover what they are doing, where they are, and where else they hang out. Look around on the Internet at different blogs, forums, and other social sharing networks to see what they are doing and where they go. This gives you a greater understanding of their mannerisms and interests, allowing you to post with greater ease and confidence because you know exactly what they are interested in. Staying on top of finding problems that your audience are having related to your niche and then solving that for them is what will differentiate you from your competition.

Business is about solving problems, so always make sure you intend to do that in the most professional and creative way possible.

Finding problems within your niche is easy to find by looking through the comments on social media pages and asking questions, showing your interest towards your audience. I've also found that researching your customers on Forums works best. For example: On Google, just simply type in (The keyword from your niche) forums – Advice needed. Doing this will come up with a load of forums of people discussing their own thoughts towards the topic, making it much easier for you to target your audience on Social media, which will then ultimately make them more intrigued towards your Instagram Page if you're answering and solving the problems they have. You can do this through posting certain quotes, certain facts and by captioning your photo to get your followers to comment and discuss their thoughts.

Reddit is an awesome way to find what your customers want and what they're having problems with.

Chapter 4: Your Image

The way your profile looks is extremely important when it comes to Instagram. This is a highly visual network that relies solely on images and image sharing to connect with your audience. While there are image descriptions and comments, the first and often only thing your audience is going to see or pay attention to are your pictures. Let's take a look at what your image is and how you can build one that will attract your audience.

What Your Audience Cares About

When it comes to Instagram, your audience cares about one thing and one thing only: the way you look. It may sound superficial, but it is the entire point of the network. In the past when Instagram was new, it was easy for businesses to share just about anything with no necessary rhyme or reason. However, modern trends in Instagram sharing have shifted, making your audience follow profiles that are visually appealing. This means that you cannot just post images that look good on their own but does not have connection or is not consistent with your overall theme. Doing so will actually result to your feed looking messy and your audience not feeling compelled to follow you. Your feed, by the way, is the collection of images you have shared on your profile.

Instead of seeing a messy feed that makes no sense, your audience wants to see a feed that has a clear reason. You should have a theme that you follow, as well as a set color scheme. You should also consider sticking to only one or two filters, to refrain from having too many different tones on your page. You can customize your filters when you share your next image by scrolling all the way to the right of the filter options, tapping the settings gear, and unselecting everything except for the one or two filters that you intend on using. This way you only have these filters available, and you do not have to scroll around to find them.

Having a clean, attractive feed makes your page visually appealing. This will create excitement within your audience, drawing them in, making them eager to look at what you have been posting. In many cases, your audience will scroll quite far back in your feed, once you have had the time to post more images, allowing them to see what your posts are about. Having a feed that is attractive and consistent gives your audience a reason to stay focused and not just click away towards your competitor who has paid attention to visual appeal.

If your posts are attractive enough and your audience is drawn in, then they may take the time to read some of the descriptions on your posts. In this case, you need to make sure that your descriptions are brief and on-point. Descriptions are where you can give a quick insight, ask for a like or share, share entertainment, or give information about a promotion you have going on.

Creating an Attractive Feed

Creating an attractive feed is not too hard, as long as you know what it is that you are trying to create. If you are unsure, take a moment to scroll back through the pages of your competitors and see what they are doing. At this time, see what colors seem to be trendy and common, as well as what themes your audience tend to use. Although choosing your own color palette and theme is important, if you choose one that is too different from what the rest of your niche is using, you may set yourself *too* far apart. In this case, your edge would become the ledge you leaped off, and your brand will become irrelevant.

When you are posting, there are four types of posts you need to be aware of: promotional, entertainment, quotes, and reposts. These types of posts are the only types you will be using; so knowing how they work, when to use them, and how to incorporate them into your feed is important.

Promotional
Promotional posts are posts that will be encouraging your audience to purchase something from you. These posts are generally made using a relevant quote or image that reflects the promotion in some way. The best way to create a promotional post on Instagram is to create a short but sweet reason for why someone would want to purchase the promotional item or service from you. While story marketing is valuable on other platforms such as Facebook, sticking to shorter post descriptions on Instagram is better. Instead of making each individual picture a story, create a story using your entire feed and build on it as you go along. You can do this by advertising your brand/ products on your posts but also using Instagram stories can catch your viewer's attention too. Taking advantage of the swipe up feature, which we will explain later on, can be a huge sales converter.

Entertainment
Entertainment posts are based on providing your audience with something interesting and entertaining to consume. These should not have any form of promotion or sales in them. On a rare occasion, entertainment and promotional posts may overlap if you post a promotional picture and then make a "sly" remark about how your product or service could fill a need being expressed in the picture.

Otherwise, these should simply be something that makes your audience smile, think, or feel interested in your content but without making them feel that they are continually being sold to. Since Instagram is heavily visual, using funny memes or other similar pictures may be enjoyable. You will need to pay attention to your audience and what they are most interested in seeing. Make sure that the topic of these posts is consistent with what you are offering and stays on-target with your niche and your brand. Entertainment posts are awesome because they get your audience commenting and liking your post. Creating a caption such as: Tag your friend who does this, or Tag a friend who agrees with this. Relating your caption towards getting your audience to tag someone is a great way to drive more traffic (people) to your page and most importantly, your business.

Quotes

Quotes are a great type of post that allows you to share insightful or interesting thoughts in an image. When done right, these images can be very inspiring and can attract the interest of your audience. If they resonate with your quotes, the audience will more likely to follow you. Furthermore, quote posts allow you to share more related insights on the ongoing story on your feed. They give you the opportunity to express your brand image in a way that the captions on your photos may not always allow since not everyone will read them. Quote images are generally best if they are shared after every two or three photos. They are often used as a way to create the design of the feed, giving you the opportunity to "break up" the imagery so that each image comes together better. You can use apps like Canva or Word Swag to gain access to the ability to create these posts on your own. Often, Instagram users will create a template on these apps and use the same one or two templates over and over on their page. This creates consistency and ensures that your feed continues to look amazing. Quotes are also good because they can get your audience commenting and tagging their friends.

Reposts
Reposts are great to share every once in a while. You can repost posts that competitors in your niche have on Instagram using special repost apps that you can install directly on your mobile device. When you do this, you can tag the person or company you are reposting. Many larger companies will use this feature to share images of their clients using their products or services or to share testimonies directly on Instagram. Others will share posts from larger businesses in the same niche as a way of staying relevant and gaining extra followers who are interested in the larger business already. Reposts should not be used excessively, but when used properly can help you massively increase your following and build stronger connections with your audience.

Organizing Them All
It is important that you know how to organize these posts in a way that appeals to your audience both visually and mentally. You want a feed that looks attractive, but you also do not want your audience to feel like you are hammering them with sales pitches all the time. Ideally, you should post approximately three times a day. During these three times, aim to post two non-sales posts and one sales post. This means you should be posting seven sales posts per week. Of those posts, make about two or three of them hard pitches and keep the rest of them as soft pitches. This means a couple of posts will directly ask for the sale whereas the others will highlight the benefits of the product

and encourage your audience to think about it or educate themselves further.

With these three posts, you also want to aim for visual appeal. Many Instagram users will have their feed arranged in a way that produces a pattern of sorts. For example, alternating quotes and images. Alternatively, they may post two images and one quote. This aligns it so that the feed has all quotes down one of the three lines and then all pictures down the other. When a potential follower then visits your page, they will see that your page is visually appealing. They will also see that it contains a lot of entertaining and fun posts, in addition to your sales posts. As a result, they will be definitely more interested in following you.

Where to Find Pictures Online

The majority of companies do not take all of their own pictures. This would be time consuming and expensive. Instead, they take pictures from the Internet to use them in their feed. Some may use the raw images they find, whereas others will filter the image so that they all have a similar look. For example, you may create a feed that is all black and white. For that reason, you would want to have a black and white filter that you use on your pictures, altering them slightly.

Finding your pictures online is quite easy. The best way is to Google Search for "royalty free stock images." There, you will find websites like Pixabay and Unsplash that contain thousands of images you can use that are free of any copyright laws. Make sure you choose images that are relevant to your own overall theme so that they stay consistent with your feed!

A Word About Copyright

Copyright infringement on Instagram is a serious issue. Being in business and getting stuck with a lawsuit around copyright can be expensive, but it can also damage your reputation online. It is important that you make sure that you choose images that are royalty-free, as this means that they do not have copyright laws on them that prevent others from using the images. If you find an image on a website or on Google that contains no information about copyright, it is important that you assume it is copy written and refrain from using it. It is always better to be safe than sorry. Most stock image websites have hundreds of thousands of images you can choose from, meaning you will always have new selections for your next post.

Post Planners

If you are looking for a really nifty way to automate your feed while also getting an idea of what it is going to look like, consider using a post planner. Apps like PLANN are great for helping you see what your feed would look like with certain images. They also allow you to schedule the posts, complete with captions and hashtags. Though, it is important that you use the hashtags in the comment section and not in the caption as this keeps your image more attractive and cleaner for the individual reading it.

Your First Post

Now that you know everything you need to do to create your feed, it is time to post your first post! Simply choose which post you want to use: promotion, entertainment, quote, or repost. Then, you can put the post on Instagram! Use a catchy caption. Then, you can go ahead and place your hashtags in the comment section. You would want to aim to have your hashtag comment posted within a few seconds after the posting, as this is what drives up engagement and gives you the best chance of getting a great result from your post. It is a good idea to pre-write your hashtags on a note in your phone and copy them so that you can simply paste them immediately after posting the photo. If you do not know how to choose your hashtags, see *"Chapter 4: Marketing Through Images,"* subsection *"Hashtags."* And, of course, make sure that you use a photograph that is attractive. If you do not have anything on your phone presently, you can always get a royalty-free one. It is important that you make sure every single photo is ultra-high quality or else people will not pay as much attention to your business. Remember, Instagram is visual-based, so you need to appeal to people's visual taste in the most attractive ways possible.

Chapter 5: Marketing Through Images

Instagram is a powerful social networking site for marketing because it revolves around images. One of the things that draw people into purchasing online is seeing the product or the results of the product or service through visual aids, such as images or videos. Since Instagram revolves around the sharing of visual aids, it gives you a unique opportunity to show your audience how incredible your products or services are, versus just talking about it.

Automation

When it comes to marketing on Instagram, there are a few other benefits you can look forward to as well, including being able to automate your posts. Automating your posts means that you can schedule days, weeks, or months in advance and simply let your automated service do the posting for you. This ensures that you are always posting three times a day with high-quality images that look good together. Remember, if you use a service like PLANN, you can also pre-arrange your images before they are even posted so that you can get the most attractive aesthetic possible. This also allows you to disperse your value, entertainment, and promotional posts throughout your feed ahead of time. If you know you are going to have a sale going on at any given point throughout the month, you can preset these posts to announce the sale for you which makes your launch and management of the sale incredibly easy.

How to Market on Instagram

Marketing on Instagram is somewhat different from other sites. On Facebook and similar pages, you can easily post longer written posts and market through storytelling. This is a great strategy to use, but on a page like Instagram, it is rendered obsolete. Since Instagram is based on visual aids, very few people actually go on to read the caption. The number of individuals who read the caption drop significantly if the caption is too long. That being said, it is essential that you get to the point fast. Ideally, your caption should be 300 characters or fewer. This gives you a great length to share a sentence or two about your product/service and then pitch the sale if it is a hard pitch post. If it is a soft pitch post, you can have 2-3 short sentences talking about how awesome your product is or highlighting the results someone is getting from it.

Marketing on Instagram is largely done through your image. Rather than writing about how awesome your product/services are, your audience wants to see it in action. Share images of people engaging in your services or using your products. If someone has left a testimony about how much they love the product, share an image of them using the product, tag them on it, and then write something like "[Client name] absolutely loved the results she gained from our product! She can't stop raving about it! To read all about why she loves it, check out her full testimony. Link in the bio!" This is short and sweet and gives those who are interested the opportunity to move over to your website. This means that they will read more about how much your customer loves the product, and then immediately click over to where they can purchase the product for themselves. This is the most effective way to share marketing posts on Instagram.

Remember, not all posts should be geared toward marketing. Share a healthy mixture of entertainment, promotion, quote, and repost so that your audience stays engaged and is more likely to browse through your promotional posts. Also, links that are posted in the caption are **NOT** clickable on Instagram. If you want someone to go to a link, always put the link in your profile and direct people there. If they are interested, they will go look.

If you're new to Instagram you want to mainly focus on providing valuable content and building up trust within your audience. You cant just start selling and promoting your business from the get go.

Hashtagging

Hashtagging on Instagram is essential. If you do not use hashtags, it is guaranteed that you are not reaching your audience. On Instagram, people search up hashtags of things they are interested in and then enjoy the images that have used that hashtag. If you want to be reaching as many people as possible, you need to use relevant hashtags. Ideally, you should include 30 hashtags on each image. Using 30 will give you the best opportunity to reach as many people as possible. Using more than 30 will result in the comment not working, as Instagram does not allow more than 30 hashtags per post.

There are two important things to remember when hashtagging your pictures. First, never put your hashtags in the caption. Always post them in the comments section. They still work, and they keep your caption clean and attractive. Second, make sure that you are not using hashtags that are too popular as you will not get seen by anyone. You also don't want to use obsolete hashtags that will barely reach anyone. This is another place where the app PLANN comes in handy. You can type in a word that you want to hashtag, and they will show you which hashtags are too popular and which ones are perfect. You can then post the ones that are best suited to reach your audience and get you seen and liked over the ones that will likely end up in your post getting buried and going unseen. While you can always use 3-4 of the more popular hashtags, avoid using too many because you'll simply waste opportunities to reach new followers.

When you are hashtagging, a great idea is to have groups of hashtags pre-written and saved in a note on your phone. Then, you can simply copy and paste the chosen group onto the comments section of your picture within a few seconds after posting. This ensures that you get "engagement" (your own comment) right away. It also ensures that you begin getting interaction quickly. If the time between you posting and receiving your first "likes" features too big of a gap, Instagram will assume you are irrelevant, and you will not be seen by as many people.

Reposts

Reposting pictures is a great way of getting seen by larger audiences. You already learned in *"Chapter 3: Your Image"*, subsection *"Reposts"* about how you can repost other people's pictures. However, you should also know that getting your own pictures reposted is highly valuable as well. When you are reposted by a company or an individual with a larger following, their posts will typically tag you as the original poster. This means that you receive exposure to their audience and a greater chance of increasing your own audience.

Getting reposted by other companies takes a bit of practice and some luck. The best way to go about it is to post exceptionally high-quality photographs, rave about the company in your caption, and tag them in the caption. You would also want to use relevant hashtags that they would be looking up. If it is a company that has their own hashtag that they like to use and encourage their audience to use, use this hashtag on your image as well. For this specific hashtag, you might want to include it in the caption so that they can see that you are using it.

When you share high-quality images that would look good on their feed, you maximize your chances of being seen. Consider looking at their feed first and seeing how your image might fit in. That way, they see your image and recognize that it would look great alongside their existing feed. This makes them more likely to repost your post and tag you for credit. If they do repost you, be sure to engage with the post and say thank you. If anyone on the post begins raving about the company, chime in and agree with how much you love them. Engaging with your audience in this way will show people that you are personable and active, making them more likely to want to follow you and engage with your profile as well.

Using these tips is a great way to get reposted by other companies. Remember, reposts are not guaranteed. However, using these tips will also help drive up your engagement on these specific posts, so even if you are not reposted, it will have a great impact on helping you tap into their following and reach a greater number of new followers.

Shout Outs

Getting shout outs on Instagram is just as valuable as getting a repost. When you get a shout out, essentially another Instagram user decides that they enjoy your content and choose to share about you in their caption. Usually, it looks something like this: "Shout out to (*your company*) and their great products that have helped me so much with (*what your product does*.)" Often, this will be shown alongside them using the product or showing off the benefits they gained from using your product or service in the image. When this happens, people get excited and eager to follow you because they already know, trust, and respect the person who shouted out to you. This means that you are far more likely to increase your reach, gain more followers, and have a greater return on your investment through Instagram. Shout outs aren't just related to the products you sell, the business page could give you a shout out thanking you for the content and value you're providing on your page and promote their audience to follow you for more information and knowledge regarding the specific niche you're both in.

When it comes to shout-outs, there is no one-way to guarantee that they will happen organically. However, you can encourage them or even pay for them. Websites like Fiverr offer services where individuals with a large following agree to shout out to your company to help drive traffic to your page. The fee for a service like this generally ranges from $5-$10 and can have a great impact on helping you grow your following, especially early on. Another option is to directly message an Instagram page related to your niche and message them saying you will give them a shout out if they give you one in return. This will work easily if the business page you are asking has a similar amount of followers as you. If they have significantly more followers than you they will ask for a payment.

Chapter 6: Getting Followers and Engagement

Aside from effective marketing, you also need to know how you can increase your followers and get more engagement on your profile. With Instagram, the number of followers you have and the amount of people who engage with your posts directly equals how many people will see your following posts. Instagram likes to share only relevant and popular content with its viewers to maximize their viewing pleasure. This is why you need to maximize your following and engagement to make sure that you stay relevant and seen by your target audience. In this chapter, we are going to discuss what you can and should do to increase your followers and maximize their engagement on your posts.

Asking for Engagement

Asking for engagements on your posts is a great and straightforward way of increasing your engagement and following. Many pages will caption their photos with something like "tag a friend who would love this!" or "who would you share this with?" Then they will often end the caption with something like "follow us for more great content!" This encourages people to think about who they could share the post with, meaning that they end up commenting and sharing your image. Since this increases your engagement, it also increases where you are seen on the Instagram "top posts" feed. Additionally, it encourages people to follow you.

Some companies will use this on almost every post, which is not necessarily a bad thing. It definitely increases engagement and following. However, it is important that you understand that customer relationships are often an important part of encouraging people to purchase from you. Make sure that you are posting additional content that encourages people to read and pay attention so that when you post a sale post, individuals are more likely to continue engaging with it. You do not want to condition your following to only engage when asked because this can result in them ignoring almost anything else you post. Creating genuine connections with your followers after asking for their engagement and follow is a great way to take full advantage of this feature and get maximum sales from Instagram marketing.

Engaging with Others

When people comment on your post, make sure that you always comment back to them. This does two things for you: it increases your customer relationships and personality, and it also shows the Instagram algorithm that you are engaging back. As well, it counts toward an additional "engagement" on your post, driving you even further up in the top posts feed that most people look at.

Engaging with others should also include you browsing the most popular hashtags that you use on your own posts and engaging with other people who post. These days, you see many people who copy and paste the same message that sounds something like this: "Great feed! You should check us out, too!" While this does count as engagement, it is not efficient. It seems very impersonal and can actually damage your customer relationships. Instead, focus on posting genuine comments. This may take more time, but it stands out and sets you apart from the rest of the individuals who are copying and pasting their engagement comments.

Giveaways

Giveaways are a phenomenal way to increase engagement and grow more followers on Instagram. They allow you to share what your products or services are, encourage people to share you with their friends and to follow your page. You get incredible benefits from your giveaways. Giveaways can be costly because they do require you to give away a free product or service, but ultimately, they are going to increase brand awareness and maximize your reach. When done right, a giveaway is ingenious and totally worth it.

The best way to facilitate a giveaway is to begin by choosing what it is that you want to give away. Pick something that will be attractive and well-liked by your audience, and that will not cost you too much. Early on, it is ideal to give away something that is going to be smaller and more affordable for you. Your engagement when your following is already somewhat small will not be at par with someone who has an already large following, so choose accordingly. Be sure to factor in shipping costs if you are shipping it to the other person as a part of what this giveaway will cost you.

Once you have chosen, take an image that captures the product or highlights the benefits of the service. Then, in your caption, post something like this: "GIVEAWAY! Want to win this FREE product? Here's how! Tag a friend, like this post, like our page, and on the last day of this month, we will draw a lucky winner! Good luck!" It is important that you format the giveaway in a way that requires individuals to tag, like, and follow you because this is how you maximize your engagement and following through a giveaway. Getting them to share your post is also ideal however, less people engage when you ask to share. If your give away is good enough it does not matter if you ask for a share.

Generating Traffic from Other Sites

This can be as passive or time-consuming as you want to make it. Some people drive traffic to their Instagram by simply posting a link to it on their Facebook, website, blog, and other online platforms. Others will actually engage with people on these other platforms and encourage them to follow the person on Instagram. How you choose to do this is entirely up to you and how much work you want to put into it. When you do engage with others and encourage them to follow you on Instagram, this is a great way to get a follower who has already built a relationship with you. Therefore they are more likely to be an engaged follower on your page.

Paid Advertisements

Instagram is one of the best platforms for posting paid advertisements. If you want to increase your following, paying for advertisements is a great way to do so. All you need to do to post a paid advertisement is choose which picture and caption you want to promote and then promote it through the "promote" button on your business Instagram account. If you have not already converted your account to a business account, you can do that by going into your settings and choosing "Switch to Business Account" and following the step-by-step walkthrough within the app.

Paid advertisements are great to use when you are announcing new products, doing a giveaway, or otherwise encouraging engagement or sales in some way on your page. When done right, they can maximize your sales or increase the engagement you actually get on the giveaway. Make sure that in setting up your advertisement, you are very specific in creating your niche so that your target audience is the one Instagram actually shows it to. Then, you can choose your budget and hit "go"! It's as simple as that!

Paid Followers

Some Instagram users like to pay for their followers as a way to quickly grow their profile and gain more interaction. Whether or not this works heavily depends on who you pay to do this and whether or not they are actually targeting the right audience. For that reason, while the increase in number of followers is guaranteed, the increased engagement is not. You want to be careful when doing this because some people may become suspicious if you have a following of 10K+ but minimal engagement on your posts. Such as 10 likes and 1 comment on your pictures.

To get paid followers on your page, simply go to a website like Fiverr. This website has many people readily willing to help you maximize your following for $5-$10. Once you pay them, you simply allow them to do their work, and within a few days' time, you will have a massive following on your account. Be sure to review the person offering to do the service before paying them so that you can verify that they are good at getting you followers and targeting the right audience. Some are better than others, so reading their reviews is important.

Using the app: Instagress also allows you to gain free followers by following other accounts. You can earn coins that will allow you to order a certain amount of followers. This can be a time consuming process and does not guarantee organic followers.

Some days you might get offered a 90% discount on 50 and 500 followers. The small payment is worth the amount of followers you get and I would recommend taking advantage of it just to get your page up to a few hundred followers.

It's important to not rely on this. You want your page to be organic, so do not get too many paid followers because when people see you have 2000 followers and you are only getting 10 likes per picture your audience will catch you out and this is not a professional look at all. Using Instagress or Fiverr for extra followers is just to get you off the ground.

- Bonus Tip: If you own a physical business, like a restaurant/food store or a clothing store etc. You can search people by location in your area on Instagram. People post pictures on Instagram and tag their location. If your business is in New York for example. Search up Places: on Instagram 'New York'. And look at the most recent pictures people are posting. Directly message them and offer them free food or a free merchandise if they visit your store today. This can sometimes be hard to swallow and allow however it works extremely well. People love free things and if you offer that to them and they then post a picture with your food/merchandise on Instagram as well as tagging your business that is cheap marketing at it's best. This can work very well, especially if the customer you offered it to has a high following.

Run through:
Step 1) Go into Instagram
Step 2) Tap into the 'Search' bar
Step 3) Click on 'Places' Tab
Step 4) Search up the location your business is in
Step 5) Look at the most recent pictures posted and message the people offering them a free giveaway if they visit you today!

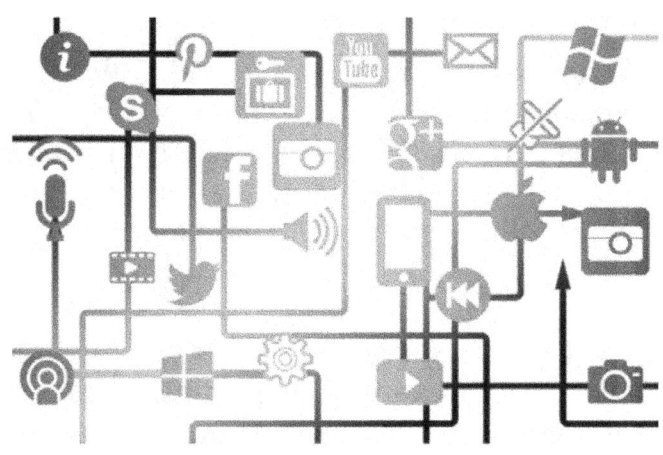

Chapter 7: Selling Your Product/Service Via Instagram

Once you have your Instagram page up and running, it's time to start generating those followers into customers! Remember don't hesitate to sell your service or products. You don't want to just consistently provide free value and knowledge without any return for yourself because at the end of the day you run a business. So now it's time to think of your plan of attack towards how you can sell your products and services within your business.

How to Get Started

If you don't already have a website set up, you can still promote your business just via Instagram. Posting photos, videos and Stories of your business in action or the products you sell is a good way to get your customers to trust you and want to buy. At the end of the day if they're following your Instagram page they have an interest in what you offer and you will convert more customers than you think as long as your provide quality value that is authentic.

Selling through Instagram Posts/ Videos

Instagram is one of the best platforms to sell on because it is Visual. If a customer sees your product or service visually through your Instagram posts or videos they will know what it's about and how it works. This is the reason most would say Instagram is the best platform to build in terms of running your business. Furthermore, Instagram offers three great ways to share with your audience, ensuring that everyone has the opportunity to see what you are sharing and selling. This includes through the feed itself, through the Instagram stories feature, and through the new IGTV (Instagram Television) feature.

Selling through Instagram Stories

Instagram stories work well if you want a customer to act right away. Stories only last 24 hours which means you have 24 hours to sell a certain product. Promoting or selling on your stories is easily done.

Selling Through Suspense:
A great selling tool that you can use on Instagram stories is generating suspense through your stories. Because they are used as a "behind the scenes" strategy, you can get your audience seeing behind the scenes features of new products or services that you are coming out with. This builds a sense of curiosity and suspense, leading your audience to wonder what they are looking at, what it will be, and when it will be released. A great example of this was when Kylie Jenner sold her lip kits using Instagram Stories as way to share their creation. For months leading up to the launch, Kylie would share behind the scenes images and videos of her in the warehouse where they were making the lips, as well as other behind the scenes elements of the project. Whenever she shared images of the colors themselves, she would share them in black and white so that all you could see was the shades and not the actual colors themselves. This resulted in her fans wondering what she was up to and curious about when they would be able to get their hands on the product. By the time they were ready to launch, Kylie gave her fans three days notice of the product finally becoming available, and sold $19 million worth of products

on day one. This resulted in her selling out of most of her products, and earning an incredible profit.

While you may not have the same massive fan-base going into your company, this does not mean you cannot take advantage of the same selling features that people like Kylie are using. Building suspense for your audience by sharing your products with them before they launch and sharing excitement with them is a great way to get people curious about what you are doing and eager to buy. Simply put: when you are excited and mysterious, your audience is excited and curious.

Using the swipe up feature:
The swipe-up feature on stories is a great way to promote anything you are currently selling. This feature makes it extremely convenient for you to add purchasing links directly in your story. This works because it prevents your audience from having to go in search of the link to purchase what you are advertising in your story. Instead, they can simply swipe up and get the sales link right there. Other people who are building their audiences are also using this as a way to share entertainment links with people, essentially teaching their audience that the "swipe up" stories on their feed are a healthy mixture of both entertainment *and* purchasable products or services. This ensures that their audience stays engaged on these posts and that they are eager and ready to purchase when the opportunity arises.

To use the swipe up feature, you do need to have a following of at least 10,000 people. Once you reach this benchmark, the feature becomes available to you and you can begin marketing to people through your stories with the swipe up setting. This setting is easy to access. When you go to create a story, you will see a new chain link button in the top right corner next to the drawing and emoji buttons on your story. Simply tap this, add your link, and your link is built! Now, all you need to do is indicate in the story that the swipe up feature has been activated. Fortunately, Instagram has also built many great stickers that you can add to your story that inform your audience to "swipe up" to see the details. Add this sticker, add the image or video to your story, and you are good to go!

Driving Instagram Traffic to your Business.

If you have a product or service you must already have a website set up. If so, Make sure the link to your website or the products are in your Instagram Bio. Mentioning in the captions of your photos: Link is in the Bio if you want this or need this. You can also ensure that your photos are branded. Many companies will add small logos or watermarks into the corners of their photographs. This makes your logo recognizable so that whenever they see your posts, your audience is reminded of what products or services you are offering and they are more likely to head over to your website and begin browsing. Another great way is to promote paid advertisements on Instagram that have the "goal" of driving visitors to your website. Though this costs money, using this feature is a great way to get seen by people in your target audience who may not already be following you. This means that they discover you, and they see the opportunity to both follow you and head over to your website to learn more about how they can purchase your products or services.

Chapter 8: Affiliate Marketing

One of the best ways to make money on Instagram if you are not making it through your own business is through affiliate marketing. Affiliate marketing is a business model that allows an individual with a larger following to market to their following for other businesses. They are given a special link or a referral code that then allows them to get paid every time one of their followers purchases a product from the company whom they are marketing for.

The great thing about affiliate marketing is that you can do it exclusively through your Instagram page. You are not required to have any business set up, meaning you are not required to maintain a website or build a brand on any other page. You can build exclusively through Instagram. The larger your following gets and the greater your engagement grows, the more likely you are to receive more people purchasing through your links. This means that you are going to earn more and more as your audience grows larger.

When affiliate marketing it is important to only promote physical or digital products that you firmly believe in and trust.

Why Choose Affiliate Marketing

Affiliate marketing is a great way of creating additional income in a manner that takes very minimal time and effort from you. When you choose this business model, you are choosing one of the most basic business models available. Rather than trying to create your own product or service, refine it, manage it, and market it, with affiliate marketing you simply have to market. This makes running your own business extremely easy and efficient. As well, you do not have to manage incoming and outgoing expenses, shipping costs, or order fulfillment. The company you are marketing for does all of that. All you do is share the product and let your audience fall in love.

A great thing about affiliate marketing is that it can become an incredible form of passive income. Most affiliate links stay active for a while, so if you create a strong post and keep it visible on your page or share it again from time to time, you increase visibility and generate money through the same link. It takes minimal effort to get great results from it.

How to Get Started

Getting started with affiliate marketing is pretty simple. If you are just starting out, you may not be eligible to get many deals directly through larger companies. However, there are companies like ClickBank that will allow you to begin creating deals with companies so that you can affiliate market with them. You can also consider using Amazon Associates Affiliate as a way to make money, as this allows you to market virtually anything that exists on Amazon.

Once you create your profile with the affiliate agent you want to use, all you have to do is get a deal with a company who is willing to let you market their products for them and pay you for it. It is important that you pay attention to what these individual's terms are because some companies will have strict terms that may prohibit you from marketing for another company at the same time. Alternatively, they may have specific requirements on how they want you to market and how often. Make sure that you are clear on what these terms are so that you can stay compliant with your agreement and do not potentially risk losing your income from that company.

It is important when setting up your agreement and choosing which companies you want to market with that you choose a company that will represent your image. Even though you are not running a complex business, you do still need to maintain an image. People who affiliate market for virtually anyone have a tendency to be seen as sleazy and very few people will actually purchase from them. However, if you have a niche and you keep your products and services on-niche and make sure that everything you share is something you can stand behind your business 100%, you increase your reputation and trustworthiness with your audience and maximize your income making ability. What you're selling has to relate to your business.

How to Market

After you have created your deal, the next step is to simply market the products that you have agreed to market. Everything regarding how you post and in what order will continue to stay the same as what we have discussed previously for those who own a business model where they are selling their own product or service. The only thing that could change anything is if you are required to post certain things or in a certain way based on the terms of your agreement.

Since affiliate links earn so much, some people do like to start a blog or another online presence that allows them to share more detailed information. Although Instagram is already an incredible tool, some people still like to maximize their return through these types of add-on. Creating a blog allows you to go more in-to-detail about your experience and what you love about the product or service and why you are promoting it. It also allows you to keep your active affiliate links organized in one place so your followers can access multiple rather than just the present thing you are promoting. Remember, Instagram only allows one link (and that's in your Instagram bio) so having a "hub"- like a website/Blog where many links can be posted may be more beneficial for you.

Chapter 9: Other Social Media

Taking Advantage of All Social media Platforms

Although Instagram is the biggest platform and has the best reach, it is also highly beneficial to use other platforms such as; Facebook, Youtube, twitter, LinkedIn, Pinsterest etc. If you can link all platforms together you can generate more traffic and followers to your Instagram.

You can increase the followers you have on on all platforms by Advertising the Social Media accounts on your Instagram Bio. Add that your username is the same as your other social media accounts. You can make a post or give away about it also. Giving away a free product or service if they tag 5 friends and follow all of your social accounts. This works great especially if what you are giving away holds value.

Resources

Here is a reminder of the resources you will need to use to help you grow your Instagram business.

Logo Design:
Fiverr, Upwork or 99 Designs (websites)

Free Images:
Pixabay and Unsplash (apps)

Instagram Post creator:
Word Dream -Text swag (free) or Word swag ($4.99) (apps)

Gaining followers and likes:
Instagress or Fiverr. (App/ Website)

Automate Instagram:
Hootsuite or PLANN (Apps)

Reposting Other Instagram pictures:
Repost (Apps)

Conclusion

Congratulations on finishing the book *"Instagram Marketing"*!

This book was designed to support you in understanding the value of Instagram and how you can use this incredible social sharing network to build brand awareness and maximize your income through online shoppers. If you were unaware of how valuable Instagram marketing was before you began reading this book, I could almost certainly guarantee that you now see how incredible this app is and how valuable it is for businesses.

I hope that in reading this book, you were able to understand not only the value of Instagram but also how you can use it in the most effective and efficient ways possible. Taking advantage of a great platform is important but knowing how to use it is essential. I hope that you now understand how you can optimize your page, create a beautiful feed that attracts your audience to you, and post in a way that increases the number of sales you make in your business. If you choose to start affiliate marketing, I hope you have a strong idea of how you can get started and what you can look forward to in your business!

The next step is to begin implementing these strategies and to stay very consistent. With online platforms, consistency is key. If you do not feel as though you are capable of remaining consistent on your own, or if you would simply like more flexibility and freedom in your schedule, do not forget that Instagram can synchronize many applications you can use to begin automating your posts. Automation is a great way to be more hands-off while still keeping your page growing and your following becoming more and more engaged. And of course, make sure you do take the time to build a relationship with your audience so that they are more inspired to purchase from you!

Lastly, if you enjoyed the book "*Instagram Marketing*" and felt that it was supportive towards creating a stronger ability to create an income through Instagram, please take the time to rate and review this book on Amazon. Your positive feedback would be greatly appreciated.

Thank you, and best of luck!

www.ingramcontent.com/pod-product-compliance
Lightning Source LLC
Chambersburg PA
CBHW071439220526
45469CB00004B/1598